Estacada Public Library
475 S.E. Main
P.O. Box 609
Estacada, OR 97023

WITHDRAWN

WITH

WATER

By Eiji Orii and Masako Orii   Pictures by Kaoru Fujishima

Estacada Public Library
475 S.E. Main
P.O. Box 909
Estacada, OR 97023

Gareth Stevens Children's Books
Milwaukee

Library of Congress Cataloging-in-Publication Data

Orii, Eiji, 1909-
    Simple science experiments with water / Eiji Orii and Masako Orii; Kaoru
Fujishima, ill.
          p. cm. — (Simple science experiments)
    Includes index.
    Summary: Presents experiments demonstrating the buoyancy of water.
    ISBN 1-555-32859-8
    1. Archimedes' principle—Experiments—Juvenile literature.
[1. Archimedes' principle—Experiments. 2. Floating bodies-
-Experiments. 3. Water—Experiments. 4. Experiments.] I. Orii,
Masako. II. Fujishima, Kaoru, ill. III. Title. IV. Series.
QC147.5.075   1989   88-23304
532'.2—dc19

North American edition first published in 1989 by

Gareth Stevens Children's Books
7317 West Green Tree Road
Milwaukee, Wisconsin 53223, USA

This US edition copyright © 1989. First published as *Ukishizumi (Let's Try Buoyancy)* in Japan with an original
copyright © 1988 by Eiji Orii, Masako Orii, and Kaoru Fujishima. English translation rights arranged with
Dainippon-Tosho Publishing Co., Ltd., through Japan Foreign-Rights Centre, Tokyo.

Additional text and illustrations copyright © 1989 by Gareth Stevens, Inc.

All rights reserved. No part of this book may be reproduced or used in any form or by any means without
permission in writing from Gareth Stevens, Inc.

Series editor and additional text: Rita Reitci
Research editor: Scott Enk
Additional illustrations: John Stroh
Design: Laurie Shock
Translated from the Japanese by Jun Amano
Technical consultant: Jonathan Knopp, Chair, Science Department, Rufus King High School, Milwaukee

1 2 3 4 5 6 7 8 9 94 93 92 91 90 89

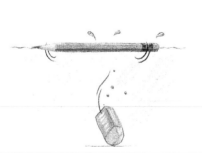

What do you know about floating and sinking?

Did you ever start to sink when you were swimming? And
did someone show you how to float? If so, you already know
something about sinking and floating.

Some light things can sink and some heavy things can float.
The same object can sink at times or float at other times. The
experiments described in this book will help you find out
more unexpected things about how water makes things sink
and float.

Look at all these vegetables! Can you guess which ones
will float and which ones will sink?

Fill a sink or a pail with water. Carefully place different fruits and vegetables in the water to find out which ones sink and which ones float.

If you put a raw egg in a glass of water, it will sink.

But some eggs float. Why?

Put one teaspoonful of salt into the water and stir. What happens if you add another teaspoonful of salt? How about if you add even more?

Gradually the egg begins to rise.

How many spoonfuls of salt do you need in order to get the egg all the way to the top of the water?

Salt water is heavier than fresh water. It will hold up more weight. This is why things float more easily in salt water.

Ask an adult for a one-quart (one-liter) bowl. Fill it with water and add four tablespoons of salt. Stir until the salt dissolves. Now carefully put three or four raw eggs in the water. Do they float? Add enough salt to make the eggs float. Which end is up? Can you guess why?

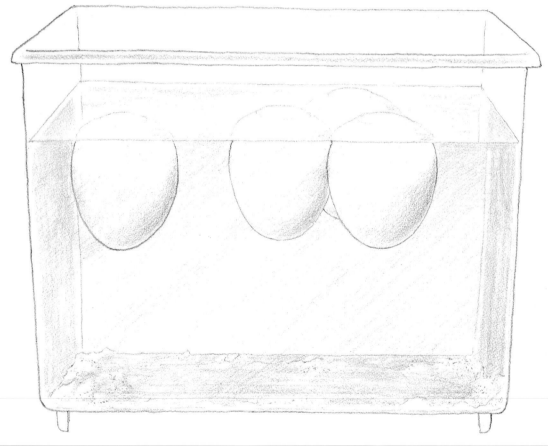

An egg floats with the bigger end up because on that end there is a pocket of air inside the shell. This makes the egg light on that end. As eggs get older, the air pocket gets larger, so you can tell when eggs are fresh. Fresh eggs will not float to the top as easily as the older ones.

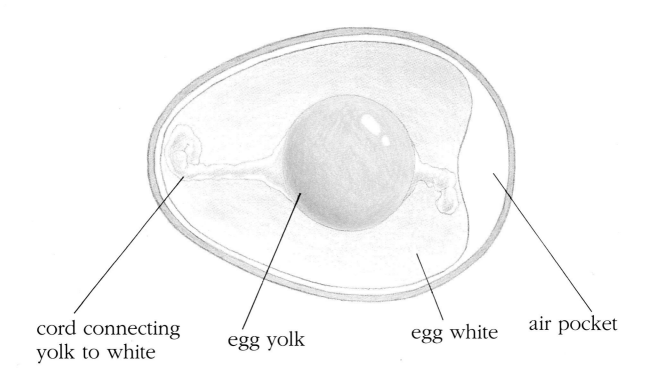

cord connecting
yolk to white

egg yolk

egg white

air pocket

Try using sugar instead of salt to make your egg float.
Add sugar a tablespoon at a time.

How about using soy sauce? Does the soy sauce make the egg float?

Put a raw egg into a glass of vinegar. What do you see?

Calcium is a mineral that makes bones, teeth, and shells
strong. Vinegar is a weak acid. The vinegar combines
with the calcium in the eggshell and produces bubbles of
carbon dioxide gas.

The bubbles surround the egg and float it up to the top.

Keep the egg in vinegar overnight. Is it still floating? The shell is soft because most of the calcium has been taken out by the vinegar.

Try leaving a grape in a light-colored soda overnight.

When the grape is covered with bubbles, it will float. The bubbles are carbon dioxide gas from the soda. This gas is what makes the soda fizz.

Try the same experiment with a raisin and a button.

A gigantic tanker sails on the sea.

Why does such a huge steel tanker float while a small vegetable, such as a potato or a carrot, will sink?

Fill a large bowl with water. Get two pieces of aluminum foil about 3 x 6 inches (8 x 15 cm) each. Crumple up one piece into a large loose wad. Carefully set the crumpled wad on the water. What happens?

Fold and roll the other piece of foil as tightly and as small as you can. Then place the tightly rolled aluminum on the water. What happens now?

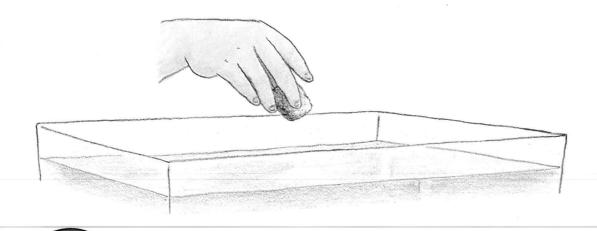

The large crumpled ball floats. It is spread out over a large area of water.

The small tight roll sinks. This is because it covers a much smaller area of water.

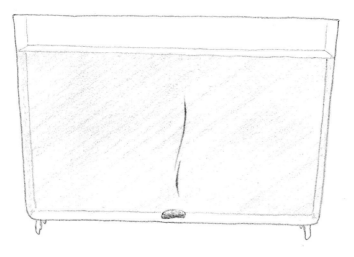

Get some plastic or rubberlike putty or clay that won't
break up in water. Pack it into a solid ball and place it on
the water. What happens?

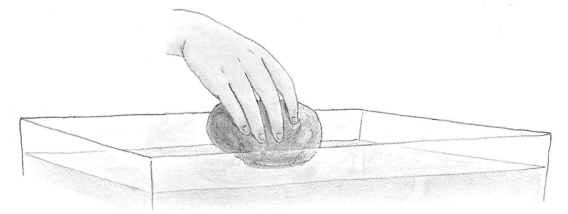

Now shape the same amount of clay or putty into a boat.
Be sure there are no places where water can come
through. Carefully set your boat on the water. What
happens this time?

The small putty ball takes the place of just a little water. This little amount of water weighs less than the ball. So the putty ball sinks.

The putty boat takes up, or displaces, much more water. The amount, or volume, of water it displaces weighs as much as the boat. So the boat floats.

Gently place a cup right side up on the water. What happens?

Now turn the cup upside down and place it on the water. What happens now?

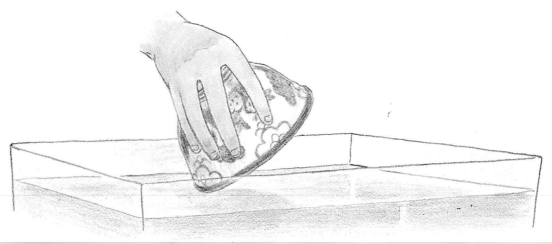

The upright cup floats.

The upside-down cup sinks.

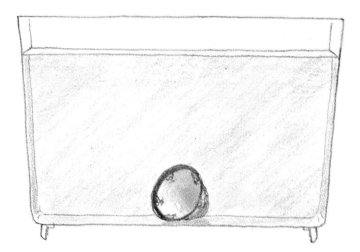

Some things will float or sink depending upon how they sit in the water.

Get two metal washers of the same size. Hang them on the ends of a small stick or pencil with thread or thin string. Tape the thread in place on the stick. Tie a flat shoelace to the middle of the stick. Slide the shoelace back and forth until the stick stays level when you hold it by the shoelace. You may want to ask an adult to help you with this.

Hold the stick level and lower one of the washers into a glass of water. What happens?

Why does the stick tip up on one end? Has the weight of the washers changed? Is something helping to hold up one of the washers?

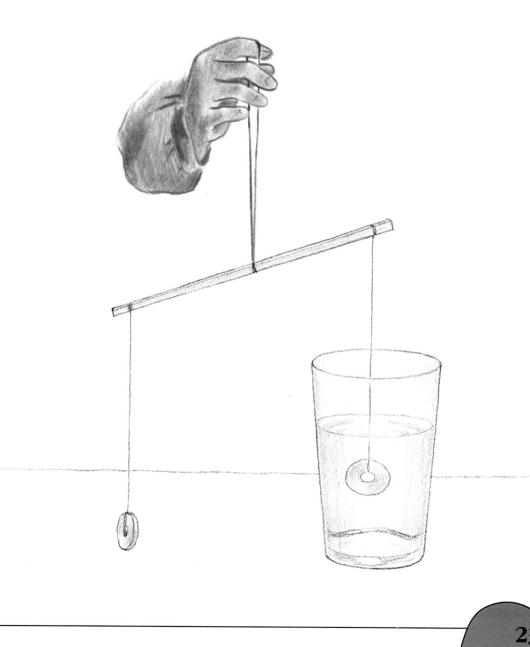

Now try putting both of the washers into the water. What happens this time?

The water in each glass helps hold up the same amount of weight in each washer. This is what makes the stick become level again.

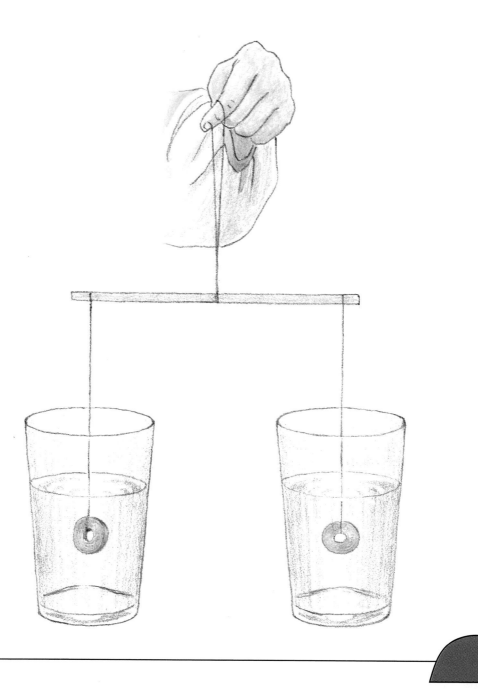

Put some salt into one of the glasses and stir. Then lower the washers into the glasses the same way that you did before. What happens?

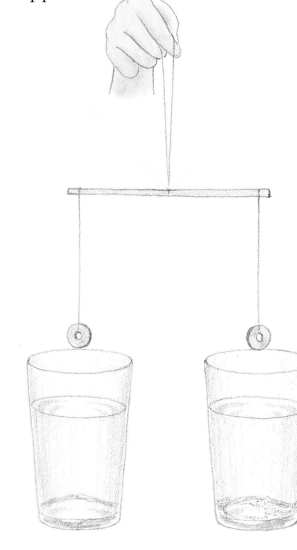

pure water   salty water

Does the salty water hold up more of the washer's weight this time?

pure water   salty water

Make two balls of clay or putty. One should be loosely rolled and the other should be tightly packed. Tie both balls to the ends of a stick. Loop a flat shoelace around the stick, and slide it to a place where the stick will hang level. Tape the shoelace in place. Fill two glasses with water. What happens when you lower both balls into water at the same time?

Which ball seems to be lighter in water — the bigger one
or the smaller one?

Archimedes and the Crown

Over 2,000 years ago, a Greek king ordered a gold crown. Later, he heard that the goldsmith used silver in place of some of the gold. The crown weighed as much as the gold the king had given to the smith. To find out the truth, the king called in Archimedes, a famous mathematician.

But one soak didn't do it. Archimedes thought for days. Then one day, as he got into his bath, he finally understood. Archimedes was so excited that he rushed into the street without his clothes!

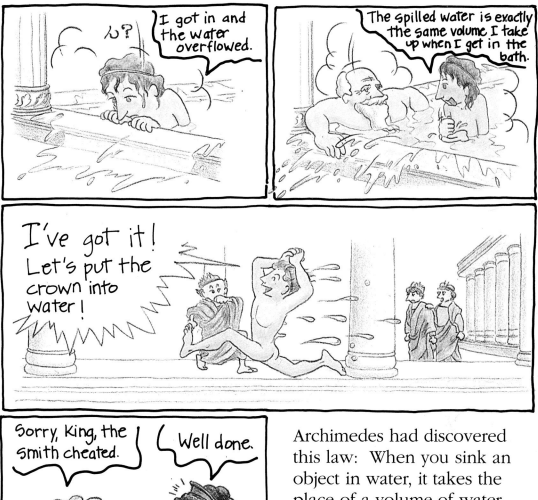

Archimedes had discovered this law: When you sink an object in water, it takes the place of a volume of water that is the same as the volume of the object. The crown displaced too much water.

GLOSSARY

Here is a list of words used in this book. After you read what each word means, you can see it used in a sentence.

Archimedes: a Greek mathematician and inventor who lived from about 287 to 212 BC
The king asked Archimedes to find out if the smith used any silver when he made the gold crown.

area: a part of any surface
The children cleaned up the mess in the play area.

calcium: an important mineral that is found in foods and needed by both humans and animals to build strong bones and teeth
Birds need calcium to form the shells of their eggs.

carbon dioxide: a gas which leaves the lungs in breathing; needed by plants in making their food; used in soda water and fire extinguishers
The fizz in soda water comes from carbon dioxide gas.

displace: to take the place of
The ship will displace more than 10,000 tons of water.

gradually: little by little, slowly
She's gradually learning her multiplication tables.

mathematician: a person who studies how numbers work
She wants to be a mathematician when she grows up.

vinegar: a sour liquid with a strong odor, used in pickling foods and in salad dressings
She put vinegar in the potato salad to make it tangy.

volume: size, amount, bulk, quantity
A baseball has greater volume than a marble.

washer: a flat disk or ring of metal that is used to keep screws tight
He put a washer under the head of each screw.

INDEX

Estac

Esta

Estacada Public Library
475 S.E. Main
P.O. Box 609
Estacada, OR 97023